Contents

Mixed Fruit Granola....2
Potato-Broccoli Soup....3
Wagon Wheel Beef Soup....4
Smoked Sausage Soup....5
Tuscan Feta Salad Sandwich....6
Oriental Beef on Rye....7
Turkey Muffuletta Pitas.... 8
Shrimp-and-Rice Salad....9
Fajita Rice Salad....10
Chicken Salad....11
Chicken Caesar Salad....12

ISBN 0-8487-2919-9
Printed in the United States of America

Mixed Fruit Granola

This sweet, fiber-rich granola can be enjoyed by itself or on top of yogurt as a quick breakfast or an afternoon snack. It's guaranteed to give you that extra boost of energy to get you through the day.

- 3 cups uncooked regular oats
- 1/4 cup wheat germ
- 1/4 cup sunflower kernels
- 1/4 cup chopped pecans
- 2 tablespoons sesame seeds
- 1/4 cup honey
- 1 tablespoon vegetable oil
- 1 teaspoon ground cinnamon
- 3/4 teaspoon vanilla extract
- Cooking spray
- 3/4 cup chopped mixed dried fruit

1. Preheat oven to 350°.

2. Combine first 9 ingredients in a large bowl. Spread mixture on a foil-lined baking sheet coated with cooking spray.

3. Bake at 350° for 20 to 25 minutes, stirring 3 times. Cool. Stir in dried fruit.

4. Store in an airtight container or pack in individual servings in zip-top snack bags up to 2 weeks. Yield: 15 servings (serving size: 1/4 cup).

***POINTS* value:** 3; Exchanges: 1½ Starch, 1 Fat
CAL 139; CARB 21.5g; FAT 5.2 (sat 0.6g); FIB 2.7g; PRO 3.9g; CHOL 0mg; SOD 3mg; CALC 20mg; IRON 1.5mg

Potato-Broccoli Soup

*Creamy, chunky, and loaded with vegetables, this nutritious soup is destined to be a lunchtime favorite. Pair it with half a ham sandwich on light wheat bread and a crisp green salad with fat-free Italian dressing for a meal with a **POINTS** value of 5.*

- 3 cups cubed peeled potato (about 1 pound)
- 1 cup frozen chopped broccoli, thawed
- ½ cup chopped carrot
- ½ cup water
- ¼ teaspoon salt
- 1 (14¼-ounce) can no-salt-added chicken broth
- 1½ cups 1% low-fat milk
- 3 tablespoons all-purpose flour
- 6 ounces light processed cheese (such as Velveeta), cubed

1. Combine first 6 ingredients in a large Dutch oven. Bring to a boil; cover, reduce heat, and simmer 20 minutes.
2. Combine milk and flour, stirring until smooth. Add milk mixture and cheese to vegetable mixture in Dutch oven. Cook over medium heat, stirring constantly, until cheese melts and mixture thickens.
3. Serve immediately, or cool and divide into individual airtight containers; refrigerate up to 3 days. Reheat in microwave. Yield: 7 servings (serving size: 1 cup).

***POINTS* value:** 3; Exchanges: 1 Starch, 1 Vegetable, 1 Lean Meat
CAL 149; CARB 21.1g; FAT 3.3g (sat 2.1g); FIB 1.7g; PRO 9.3g; CHOL 12mg; SOD 658mg; CALC 216mg; IRON 0.8mg

Wagon Wheel Beef Soup

*A handful of pantry staples comes together to create this hearty, down-home soup. Use assorted shapes of pasta and different beans to add variety. For a lunch with a **POINTS** value of 5, serve with 6 saltine crackers and an apple.*

- 3 cups wagon wheel pasta
- Cooking spray
- ¾ pound ground round
- 1 cup frozen chopped onion
- ½ teaspoon dried oregano
- 1 (1-pound, 10-ounce) bottle low-fat pasta sauce
- 1 (16-ounce) can red kidney beans, undrained
- 2 (14-ounce) cans less-sodium beef broth (such as Swanson)

1. Cook pasta according to package directions, omitting salt and fat.

2. Heat a Dutch oven coated with cooking spray over medium-high heat. Add beef and onion; cook until beef is browned, stirring to crumble. Drain well, and return beef mixture to pan. Add cooked pasta, oregano, and remaining ingredients. Cook over medium-high heat until thoroughly heated.

3. Serve immediately, or cool and divide into individual airtight containers; refrigerate up to 3 days or freeze up to 1 month. Reheat in microwave. Yield: 8 servings (serving size: 1½ cups).

***POINTS* value:** 3; Exchanges: 1½ Starch, ½ Medium-Fat Meat
CAL 160; CARB 22.1g; FAT 2.9g (sat 1.1g); FIB 3.0g; PRO 11.2g; CHOL 10mg; SOD 471mg; CALC 28mg; IRON 2.2mg

Smoked Sausage Soup

*For a filling lunch with a **POINTS** value of 4, serve with a large green salad with fat-free salad dressing and 4 short crispy breadsticks.*

- 1 teaspoon olive oil
- 1 (14-ounce) package low-fat smoked sausage, sliced
- 1½ cups finely chopped onion
- ½ cup finely chopped celery
- ½ cup finely chopped carrot
- 2 garlic cloves, minced, or 2 teaspoons bottled minced garlic
- 1 (32-ounce) carton fat-free, less-sodium chicken broth
- 1 (14.5-ounce) can diced tomatoes, undrained
- ⅓ cup uncooked long-grain rice
- ½ teaspoon salt
- ½ teaspoon pepper
- 1 (7-ounce) bag fresh baby spinach

1. Heat oil in a Dutch oven over medium-high heat. Add sausage and next 4 ingredients; sauté 4 minutes or until vegetables are tender.
2. Add chicken broth and next 4 ingredients; bring to a boil. Cover, reduce heat, and simmer 15 minutes or until rice is done. Remove from heat; stir in spinach.
3. Serve immediately, or cool and divide into individual airtight containers; refrigerate up to 3 days or freeze up to 1 month. Reheat in microwave. Yield: 8 servings (serving size: 1 cup).

***POINTS* value:** 2; Exchanges: 1 Starch, 1 Lean Meat
CAL 132; CARB 18.0g; FAT 2.5 (sat 0.7g); FIB 2.5g; PRO 11.5g; CHOL 17mg; SOD 897mg; CALC 48mg; IRON 1.3mg

Tuscan Feta Salad Sandwich

*Make this sandwich at night so it's ready for the next day's lunch. Use a very dense bread so your sandwich doesn't get soggy. Add 1 cup of fresh melon for a satisfying lunch with a **POINTS** value of 7.*

- 1 (8-inch) round loaf sourdough bread
- 1/4 cup fat-free balsamic vinaigrette
- 2 cups thinly sliced romaine lettuce
- 1 cup sliced tomato (about 1 large)
- 1 (4-ounce) package crumbled feta cheese
- 1 1/4 cups sliced peeled cucumber (about 1 medium)
- 1/2 cup sliced red onion
- 1/4 cup sliced ripe olives

1. Cut bread in half horizontally. Hollow out top and bottom halves of bread, leaving 1-inch-thick shells; reserve torn bread for another use. Brush inside of bread shells with 3 tablespoons vinaigrette. Layer lettuce and tomato in bottom half of bread shell; brush tomato with remaining vinaigrette. Layer cheese, cucumber, onion, and olives over tomato. Replace top half of bread shell. Wrap tightly in plastic wrap; chill up to 8 hours. Cut into wedges to serve. Yield: 6 servings (serving size: 1 wedge).

***POINTS* value:** 6; Exchanges: 2 1/2 Starch, 1 Vegetable, 1 Fat
CAL 273; CARB 43.0g; FAT 6.8g (sat 3.4g); FIB 3.6g; PRO 9.8g; CHOL 17mg; SOD 896mg; CALC 172mg; IRON 2.6mg

Oriental Beef on Rye

Go on—make your co-workers jealous when you pull this flavorful sandwich out of your lunch bag. Broccoli florets, light ranch dressing, and fresh pineapple chunks round out the meal for a ***POINTS*** value of 7.

2	tablespoons fat-free mayonnaise
2	tablespoons low-sodium teriyaki sauce
2	teaspoons minced peeled fresh ginger
1	garlic clove, minced, or 1 teaspoon bottled minced garlic
6	(1-ounce) slices rye bread
½	cup arugula or spinach
2	tablespoons sliced almonds, toasted
9	ounces thinly sliced 98%-fat-free deli roast beef

1. Combine first 4 ingredients, mixing well. Spread 1 teaspoon mayonnaise mixture on each of 3 bread slices. Arrange arugula and almonds on top. Drizzle each sandwich with 1 teaspoon mayonnaise mixture. Arrange roast beef evenly on sandwiches. Drizzle each sandwich with 1 teaspoon remaining mayonnaise mixture; top with remaining bread slices. Wrap each sandwich in plastic wrap, and chill at least 1 hour. Yield: 3 servings (serving size: 1 sandwich).

***POINTS* value:** 5, Exchanges: 2½ Starch, 1½ Very Lean Meat
CAL 225; CARB 40.4g; FAT 3.8g (sat 0.1g); FIB 3.4g; PRO 10.9g; CHOL 23mg; SOD 979mg; CALC 75mg; IRON 1.6mg

Turkey Muffuletta Pitas

Photo on cover

Mix up the tangy filling for this pocket sandwich in advance. Pack the filling, lettuce, and pita separately in your lunch bag. When you're ready to eat, put the sandwich together, and you've got a lunch in seconds! For a ***POINTS*** *value of 2, baked chips (1 ounce) and celery sticks are a delicious addition to these stuffed pitas.*

- 3 ounces thinly sliced smoked turkey, cut into strips
- 2 ounces thinly sliced provolone cheese, cut into strips
- 1½ cups finely chopped red bell pepper
- ⅓ cup sliced pimiento-stuffed olives
- ¼ cup chopped fresh parsley
- 2 tablespoons fat-free Italian dressing
- 2 tablespoons red wine vinegar
- 3 small garlic cloves, minced, or 1 tablespoon bottled minced garlic
- 1 cup shredded lettuce
- 2 (6-inch) pitas, cut in half

1. Combine first 8 ingredients in a medium bowl; toss well. Cover and chill at least 1 hour.

2. Spoon lettuce evenly into pita halves. Spoon turkey mixture evenly on top of lettuce. Yield: 4 servings (serving size: ½ pita).

POINTS **value:** 4; Exchanges: 1 Starch, 1 Vegetable, 1 Very Lean Meat, ½ Medium-Fat Meat
CAL 196; CARB 25.2g; FAT 6.2g (sat 2.5g); FIB 2.6g; PRO 11.0g; CHOL 18mg; SOD 675mg; CALC 161mg; IRON 2.1mg

Shrimp-and-Rice Salad

*This main-dish salad is a great make-ahead lunch or dinner. For a lunch with a **POINTS** value of 7, serve with fresh orange wedges.*

- 1 pound medium shrimp, cooked and peeled
- 3 cups cooked basmati rice (about 1 cup uncooked)
- 2 cups chopped seeded tomato (about 2 large)
- 1 cup chopped green bell pepper (about 1)
- 1/2 cup medium pitted ripe olives, halved
- 1/3 cup fresh lemon juice
- 2 tablespoons chopped fresh dill
- 2 tablespoons olive oil
- 1 teaspoon salt
- 1/4 teaspoon freshly ground black pepper
- 2 garlic cloves, minced, or 2 teaspoons bottled minced garlic
- 1/2 cup (2 ounces) crumbled feta cheese

1. Combine first 5 ingredients in a large bowl; toss well. Combine lemon juice and next 5 ingredients; stir well with a whisk. Pour dressing over rice mixture; add cheese, tossing gently to coat. Cover and chill at least 2 hours. Yield: 6 servings (serving size: 1 1/3 cups).

***POINTS* value:** 6; Exchanges: 2 Starch, 1 Vegetable, 1 Medium-Fat Meat, 1 Fat
CAL 278; CARB 34.0g; FAT 9.5 (sat 2.9g); FIB 1.8g; PRO 15.0g; CHOL 101mg; SOD 734mg; CALC 101mg; IRON 2.5mg

Fajita Rice Salad

Transform lunch into a lively, south-of-the-border feast with a ***POINTS*** *value of 6: Serve over lettuce leaves with 1 cup grape tomatoes, ½ cup pico de gallo, and 1 (8-inch) soft flour tortilla.*

- 3 cups cooked instant brown rice (about 1 cup uncooked)
- 1¼ cups chopped lean ham
- ½ cup chopped celery
- ¼ cup chopped red onion
- 3 tablespoons chopped ripe olives
- ¼ cup light mayonnaise
- 2 tablespoons fresh lime juice
- 1½ teaspoons fajita seasoning

1. Combine first 5 ingredients in a large bowl; toss well. Combine mayonnaise, lime juice, and fajita seasoning in a small bowl; stir well. Add mayonnaise mixture to rice mixture; toss well to coat. Cover and chill. Yield: 4 servings (serving size: about 1⅓ cups).

POINTS **value:** 4; Exchanges: 1 Starch, 1 Vegetable, 1 Very Lean Meat, ½ Medium-Fat Meat
CAL 196; CARB 25.2g; FAT 6.2g (sat 2.5g); FIB 2.6g; PRO 11.0g; CHOL 18mg; SOD 675mg; CALC 161mg; IRON 2.1mg

Chicken Salad

Surround a scoop of herbed Chicken Salad with 1 cup of seasonal fruit and 6 saltine crackers for a lunch with a ***POINTS*** *value of 7.*

1¾ cups chopped cooked chicken breast
⅓ cup diced celery
¼ cup finely chopped green onions
¼ cup reduced-fat mayonnaise (such as Hellmann's)
3 tablespoons chopped fresh parsley
2 tablespoons plain fat-free yogurt
1 tablespoon fresh lemon juice
½ teaspoon salt
½ teaspoon dried basil
¼ teaspoon pepper
1 (2-ounce) jar diced pimiento, drained

1. Combine all ingredients in a bowl; stir well. Cover and chill up to 2 days. Yield: 4 servings (serving size: ½ cup).

POINTS **value:** 3; Exchanges: ½ Starch, 3 Very Lean Meat
CAL 139; CARB 7.0g; FAT 3.3g (sat 0.6g); FIB 0.8g; PRO 19.7g; CHOL 52mg; SOD 493mg; CALC 31mg; IRON 1.0mg

Chicken Caesar Salad

This large, single-serving salad is ideal for a brown-bag lunch; toss the salad with croutons, dressing, tomato, and cheese just before serving. For a meal with a ***POINTS*** *value of 6, serve with 1 cup of sweet sliced strawberries.*

- ½ (6-ounce) package refrigerated grilled-flavored chicken breast strips (such as Louis Rich Carving Board)
- 2 cups torn romaine lettuce
- ¼ cup sliced peeled cucumber
- ¼ cup fat-free Caesar-flavored croutons
- 2 tablespoons low-fat creamy Caesar dressing (such as Just 2 Good!)
- 1 small plum tomato, quartered
- 1 tablespoon preshredded fresh Parmesan cheese

1. Combine chicken strips, lettuce, and cucumber in a bowl; toss gently. Add croutons and dressing; toss well. Top with tomato wedges, and sprinkle with cheese. Yield: 1 serving (serving size: 3 cups).

***POINTS* value:** 5; Exchanges: 1 Starch, 1 Vegetable, 3 Lean Meat
CAL 242; CARB 19.5g; FAT 7.4g (sat 2.8g); FIB 2.8g; PRO 25.4g; CHOL 71mg; SOD 1,306mg; CALC 134mg; IRON 2.4mg